Voices of Cyn...

Traces of a Backslider

Cynthia Evans

Published by NCM Publishing.

For information regarding special discounts or bulk purchases, please contact NCM Publishing at orders@ncmpublishing.com.

Unless otherwise noted, scripture quotations are taken from the King James Version of the Holy Bible.

Copyright © 2011 by NCM Publishing
ISBN 978-0-9833461-4-2
Library of Congress Catalog Card Number: 2011941046

Voices of Cyn...Traces of a Backslider
Written by: Cynthia Evans
Edited by: Ronald Evans, Leila Jefferson, David Good – *The Editing One*
Text Formation: Write On Promotions, Cynthia Evans, Ronald Evans
Cover Design and Layout: Brand Concepts Creative Media
Cover Photographs: Robert John Kley,
        www.rjkphoto.com

Printed in the United States of America.

Jeremiah 2:19

Thine own wickedness shall correct thee, and thy backsliding shall reprove thee: know therefore and see that it is an evil thing and bitter, that thou hast forsaken the Lord thy God, and that my fear is not in thee, saith the Lord God of hosts.

Dedication

I dedicate this book to my beloved brothers, Tyrece, Terence, and Tier Dickson, Demar and Charles Cook Jr. I pray that as you embrace your own journey you will seek God for wisdom and direction. The enemy has a plan to destroy each of you but God has a greater plan. I trust that His plans for you will prevail. I also dedicate this book to the backslider. Not everything I discuss herein will pertain to your specific situation and not everything that you may be facing will be included. However, I pray that by reading my testimony you are encouraged to try God again. Live for Christ no matter what it is that you may go through during this lifetime. May God continue to bless and keep you.

Contents

Foreword

There was that day, that moment, that split second or even that year when it seemed that going back just might have been the better option. The road ahead was dark or appeared impossible to navigate and the security and comfort of those familiar places was loudly calling. The remnants of our past, what we used to be or used to do, make a strong attempt to resurface into our present and future. I think we have all been at that place before and maybe someone reading this book is there right now.

As you read on Cynthia will share with you much of what has made her the woman she is today; the woman God can use for His glory, the woman I love, the loving mother of our children, the best friend anyone could have, the student of higher education, the encourager and minister of the good news of Jesus Christ. She will tell you it has been a laborious process reaching this place; I am a witness to that fact. Please note, however, that the process is universal. We all are evolving and must make the necessary adjustments to our behavior and character as God takes us from spiritual infancy to maturity.

- Ronald Evans

Acknowledgements

I give honor to God, who is the head of my life.

To the love of my life, my husband Ronald Evans, who is the head of my home. Your love for me and patience with me has helped me to endure my process of development in order that I may become the helpmeet that you deserve and the woman God has created me to be. You are the wind beneath my wings.

To my amazing stepchildren, Charmaine & Timothy Evans, I am thankful that we are in a good place in our relationship. I pray the blessings of God over your life. I trust that my transparency will help you make better choices than I did and avoid having to take life's detours and be delayed in reaching God's designed destiny and purpose for your life.

To my phenomenal son, Jason Hymes, Jr., you have been the best part of my life. You have witnessed and endured a lot. Because of you, I strive to be better and I am so proud to be your mom. To my granddaughter, Jamonni Williams, you are so beautiful and talented. God has graced you with many inherent gifts. I pray that as you grow, you choose to utilize those gifts in His kingdom.

To my guardian angels Uncle Otis, Aunt Virtie, Grandma Jean, and Godmother Carolyn Peoples, thank you for always being there for me; I love you eternally.

To my best friend, Nicole Knight, I love you with everything that is in me. We have come a long way and I am glad that we are on this journey together. To Arrick Foster, Priscilla Henderson and Christin Utley, you have been my confidants and great supporters and I love you dearly. A special thank you to Ni'cola Mitchell and NCM Publishing. Ni'cola, it has been an honor working with you on this project. Thank you for your hard work, love, and support. To my NCM Publishing Family *Let's Go Get'em!*

Finally and most importantly, to every backslider who wants to come home. God is waiting for you. Be of good cheer and of good courage. Know that there is no place like home.

I Love You with the Love of Christ,

- *Cynthia Evans*

In Loving Memory of

Janice Marie Claiborne

November 16, 1955 - September 21, 2011

Rest in Paradise

Voices of Cyn...

Traces of a Backslider

Cynthia Evans

Prologue

Chemistry

This is crazy. Simply insane. The way my body jolts at just the mention of your name. The chemistry engaged between you and me that had us both rejoicing. We were forcing something that was never meant to be because we needed more than chemistry to be a couple.

We need more than just the intertwining of our bodies, the locking of our lips or the dips and shifts; more than just heavy breathing from the explosion of full pleasure. We cannot measure the quality of our relationship off pure ecstasy. Ecstasy is supposed to feel good but it does not last forever.

Nevertheless, that pleasure does not override the pain. It does not cover up the black eyes or the blood that drains out of my veins. It does not take back the hurtful words and deeds that invade my mind every time I think about our chemistry.

Chemistry nearly killed me. It beat me upside my head like a punching bag and dragged me across the floor. It stomped me as if I were a whore who tried to run away from her pimp. It tempted me to return the favor.

If I could just come out of this shock, I would rock your world. I would drop chemistry and add mathematics. You know, I never really liked science anyway. I would have my way with you. Two minus one equals me without you and I could live with that.

I could live without the dangers you brought into my life. To think, I actually thought about becoming your wife. How trifling is that? How desperate was I? Chemistry was a lie.

It deceived me into thinking you were the man of my dreams. The one who made me scream with joy until that scream derived from something I never imagined. I never dreamed you could hit me like that. I never knew that I would be that cat who went back after the abuse and the threats. But, I did.

Chemistry was like, *Please! We can get through this. It was just one of those unfortunate incidents.* You know none of this makes sense since Chemistry was venomous.

The kind of toxin that had me doing the unthinkable... the unbelievable.

I still cannot believe I let your sperm meet my eggs; making babies I never had. And I know what I did was wrong but I just would not do right. Right meant that Chemistry would be in my life for at least another eighteen years. I just had to keep Chemistry out of my life.

Lord, please forgive me.

Chemistry.

Luke 15:7

I say unto you, that likewise joy shall be in heaven over one sinner that repenteth, more than over ninety and nine just persons, which need no repentance.

Cynthia Evans

Introduction

I have often wondered why it is that I was faced with many of the circumstances of my life. I do not believe I did anything to deserve being abandoned by my father, having a mother who struggled with addictions and abdicated the raising of my three younger brothers to me, forcing me to grow up way too soon in many ways. I did not sign up for a life in the projects of Chicago, dodging bullets, avoiding gang wars and devaluing my own worth to a sexual level. But I am now certain that there was a reason for every season of my life. Tactics the enemy used in an attempt to destroy me were only allowed by God to build my testimony for His redeeming power.

I now know that I was never alone even though at times I could not feel God's presence through the darkness and the pain and the tears. He was there through it all, making the way of escape for me, orchestrating the events of my life to lead me right into the place where I could shine as an example of His faithfulness and transforming power.

The writings that follow were a labor of love that required me to revisit some of the most difficult places in my journey; places that I never desired to see again. I have cried afresh as I recalled the fears, betrayals, foolishness and struggles along this journey. However, I have also marveled at God's goodness and mercy that undoubtedly has followed me all the days of my life.

I pray that as you read on you will begin to see that you are also not alone. God has not forsaken you. Trust that there is purpose behind your pain. God will show up. Maybe my sharing with you some of my struggles will help you make better choices than I did. Like every other Christian, whether they will admit it or not, I am a sinner saved by grace. I have prayed to the Lord to forgive my transgressions and I believe that He has forgiven every one of them. As I come into greater knowledge of Christ and begin to love the Lord as He loves me I understand more and more that what I have done in my ignorance does not have to hold me hostage and prevent me from becoming who God has designed me to be.

The Word of God tells me that I shall be *the head and not the tail, above and not beneath.* God has declared that I am *fearfully and wonderfully made.* I am a child of the King. The Bible also clearly speaks to the fact that Jesus died for my sins and that in Christ I am *free from the law of sin and death.* Therefore, I ignore anyone who tries to keep me bound in my past sins. God has forgiven me, in that same spirit, I have to forgive others, and I pray that others will forgive me as well.

Let me be honest, initially I was eager to write a book that would speak to the backslider. I became excited about being able to note related scriptures and minister words of encouragement but God had another plan for the direction of this book. To my surprise, He had me be more transparent than I intended about my own incidents of backsliding. I submitted to the will of the Lord and now present to you *Voices of Cyn...Traces of a Backslider.*

While writing this material I came to understand that the only way anyone would be impacted by my testimony would be for me to actually *give* the testimony. I realized that I would have to dig deeper than the surface. I pushed through my pain of recollection and embarrassment to give you all that I have. I must warn you that I did not always know the right answers. I also have to acknowledge that many times I did the wrong things even when I may have known better. I confess I do not always *practice what I preach* like some of you reading this might do. Honestly, it is easier for me to tell someone else what to do and hold them accountable for their actions or lack thereof, than it is to keep myself on the right track. One of the most challenging obstacles I experience is the governing of me.

My hope is that this book will speak to those who find themselves wavering in their faith, sliding back into the familiar and being apprehensive about walking in the gifts God has given to them because of their imperfections. You must know that this is not an *all or nothing* endeavor, as the enemy would have you to believe. There are familiar scriptures from the Word of God used throughout the text to both challenge and encourage us along the way.

The purpose of this book is to let those of us who may have, at times, turned back, questioned our faith or felt unworthy of God's favor because of our failures, know that God loves sinners but He wants sinners to strive to live righteously. Paul asked the question, *Shall we continue in sin that grace may abound?* God knew when He chose us that there would be a series of bumps in our road. But He did not design the obstacles to destroy us, nor did He give them the power to take us out. The obstacles are to keep us seeking Him, in seeking Him, we become stronger and in experiencing each victory, we become a greater representation of God's glory. Please understand that every one of us needs God operating in our lives and on our behalf.

The Lord gives us all free will. We can freely live for Christ and reap the blessings of eternal life, or we can freely choose the alternative – living to satisfy the selfish desires of our flesh - and reap the sorrows of eternal death. Repentance from sin is optional but it is necessary if we intend to be a part of the kingdom of heaven. I want heaven to rejoice and be glad over you and me. I pray that as we go through this journey of Christian living together that we hold one another up in prayer and hold each other accountable to living for Christ.

The Search for Love

As the saying goes, "When you know better you do better". If you had to give your spiritual life an age, how old would you be? Based on my birth into this world I would be thirty-two at the time of writing this book. Based on the time of my spiritual re-birth I would be around sixteen. When I look at the condition of my flesh and the state of my carnal mind, sometimes I feel like I need to get saved all over again and start fresh, but I believe in God's eyes I am right where I need to be to give Him glory. I am not proud of it but the reality is that I have been very inconsistent in my spiritual development, in and out of the church since I was first saved. I was either all the way in and on fire for Jesus or I was all the way out and kicking it good on the devil's territory. I know how to put on a dress or suit to cover up the goodies and look saved when I want to and I know how to step out as the embodiment of sinful pleasure. Whichever road I was on at the time I was rolling at full speed. Somewhere along the way, I came to realize that switching back and forth was getting me nowhere fast. I had to make up my mind and choose to live for Christ.

Although it might be *easier said than done* we must *do* the will of the Lord when it is simple or when it is a challenge and let us be real, it is challenging at times. It is during the challenges that our faith is tested and proven. The challenges help to build our strength and our character. At some point we all must realize and accept the fact that we cannot serve both God and satan. I thank God for the Holy Spirit because when I find myself yielding to the desires of my flesh in order to feel good at the expense of my obedience to God I am convicted immediately. Sometimes I am not convicted until I am in the midst of my mess but the conviction often comes before I even get started, while I am planning it in my head. As I mature in Christ, I am learning to yield to the Holy Spirit's conviction instead of following through with what my flesh wants. Historically, most of the time, I still did what I wanted to do anyway, when I wanted to do it.

How does somebody step outside the will of God on purpose? That is the place where I found myself more often than I like to think about. We deliberately disobey God yet we proclaim that we love Him with all of our heart, all of our soul and with *everything that is within us*. We pray a quick *Lord forgive me* when we are done, run to church on Sunday to hear a good Word and be saved all over again. We stay saved until next weekend then do it all again. We are not reverencing God when we defy him. So we must ask ourselves, if we love Him with all that is within us then what is in us? Do we even know what love is?

I believe the absence of real true Godly love leaves a void that has to be filled. If that void is not filled with the love of God and strong loving relationships then it will be filled with something else. If the correct concepts about love are not taught and modeled early in life then perverted concepts and perceptions of love are allowed to take up residence in our heart. These perverted concepts can plague our lives and damage our ability to recognize and be consistently committed to the right and healthy path. It was not until recently that I began to understand just how significantly my emotions and behaviors have been impacted by my early twisted love relationships. My life experiences with others such as my parents, past relationships with men, family and friends have shaped my style of interaction with people on all levels. Prior to learning and understanding love in the biblical sense I often confused the term love with lust and with a *ride or die* kind of commitment. For me love was more of a feeling than the action that demonstrated its presence.

As I grew older, I perceive that my definitions of love have changed over time. I used to define love as this unexplainable feeling that just is an expression of one's true feelings, an emotion that has a mind of its own or a disease without a cure. Wow, I actually compared love to a disease! It is interesting how you can measure a person's spiritual maturity by the way they define certain concepts. Recalling how I once defined love shows me how little I knew about real love. How could I have compared something so amazingly beautiful and worthy of being cherished to a disease? Obviously, my concept of love had been polluted and perverted.

I can tell you today that God is Love. He gave His only son to become sin for us, to die in our place so that we could have everlasting life. So today, when someone asks me the question *What is love?* My response is simple *Jesus.* You will never know what true love is until you come to know Jesus Christ. Before I fell in love with Jesus I was looking for what I thought was love in all the wrong places to fill the huge void in my life. I soon learned that many times when I thought I was receiving love from a man it was usually an illusion. It was not the real thing. One such relationship inspired me to write my feelings down and I share those feelings with you in the following poem titled *All in My Head.*

All in My Head

I remember the day we met.

Our eyes met and I felt nothing. Nothing but flattery that you showed interest and that interest fed the ego of a person who wanted so badly to be noticed.

I remember when you started hanging around a lot. I thought *this feels good.* Just maybe I could see myself in your arms, embracing your charm and wondering if this could be real. Then it happened.

One day I looked up and found myself wanting you back. I wanted you the way you wanted me when you first pursued me but the transfer of power came and sent me on an emotional rollercoaster that nearly devastated me.

You started saying that I was crazy. Lying about the days you spent in my presence because your eyes had caught another. And I remember the day y'all met. Your eyes met and again I felt nothing.

Nothing but betrayal and misery, flustered that you transferred your feelings. Just like that, you transferred our dealings and began to play chess with the dark angel. An angel in disguise but a perfect match for you. The person you thought would spend forever with us. The one you trusted while you lusted after me day by day.

Round and around this merry-go-round, up and down this rollercoaster. Transition after transition, confusion, disconnection from reality; ingrained in the desire to *win;* to make real the fantasy that was all in my head.

You were not going to leave me spinning out of control. My motivation was the memory of when our eyes first met. I remember the smile that rose on your face every time I walked by. I remember but somehow you forgot. I just had to make you remember.

I tried harder and harder; yet, we grew farther and farther apart. My heart wept, my eyes cried blood and the life I had grown to love was no more. You forgot that you misled me into thinking that I was the *one*. You had me running around town looking like the fool that I was. Distressed trying to repress what I was really feeling. It was a mess. I was a mess but now it is all good.

It is all good because the hurt and pain that drained my soul brought to life a gift I never knew existed. I began to put a pen to a pad. Line after line I spilled my guts. I cried out to whoever would listen and I wrote about us. Actually, I wrote about me.

I wrote about a person who loves hard and is a fighter. A passionate individual, who perseveres through adversity and that, my friend, is not just in my head I have already proven it. It is who I am and I thank you. I thank you for bringing out the best in me.

I *win* every day I awake and my feet hit the floor, every day that I go on with thoughts of you no more.

All in My Head

I had fallen in love for the first time, or so I thought, with a man a few years my senior. I had freely given him my virginity. In the name of love, I gave away what God had designed to be shared between husband and wife. How could I have parted with this special gift so carelessly? You see the impact of experiences and exposures during the early stages of life are often underestimated. I was doing what I thought I needed to do to feel the feelings of love, desire, admiration and attention. I was wanted. I was good.

My mom, who was entangled in a web of addiction, drowning down the tubes of her crack pipe, had not even noticed that her beautiful, blossoming, impressionable and naive teenage daughter had been sexing a grown man right in her bedroom and in her bed. The bed she shared with men she brought home. I was only doing what I had seen her do with them as my curiosity drove me to look through her bedroom keyhole. *So, that is what men like huh? Touching him there drives him crazy does it? Then you turn around and let him do that? They act as if it feels good. Okay, I am going to try all of this the first chance I get. They keep coming back for more. This must be the way to keep a man.* I began to believe that love was more than a word, it was apparently an action displayed through sexual intercourse too.

So here I am, a teenager *in love* with a man who is just playing with my mind, engaging in hot, passionate sex, not love making, but sex. I was acting out all of those lustful fantasies I developed as I watched my mom do it; and came up with some moves that momma did not teach me. I figured the better I was at it and the more I gave him these physical expressions of my love, that he would love me all the more. Consequently, my search for love through men became one of my biggest strongholds. I found myself always searching for chemistry. My man had to make me feel a certain way or hit the road. I equated love with chemistry. If the chemistry was there so was I... ride or die, and from reading the prologue, you see where *Chemistry* got me. Although I was working at filling my void in the physical sense, the emptiness was still there due to a lack of healthy relationships in my life.

As I continued my search for love, I found myself sixteen years old and homeless. I met an older man during one of my stays in Las Vegas. He had taken an interest in me. Either he was very sympathetic to my troubled upbringing or pathetically intent on having sex with someone he probably thought was fresh meat. He told me upfront that he was separated from his wife. *Who cares?* I thought to myself. Besides, being with a married man was acceptable in the home where I was raised. My mom had been seeing a married man on a regular basis.

Initially I was not attracted to this man, but he became my *knight in shining armor* the day my mom kicked me out of the house, *yeah that is a story all by itself.* He provided me with a roof over my head, food to eat and money to spend. The inevitable happened; I turned up pregnant with his child. Sixteen and pregnant for the first time, he was able to persuade me to abort the pregnancy. It turned out that he and his wife were, in actuality, not so separated after all. She too was pregnant. When I confronted him with it, he became violent and began to pound me in my face as if I were a punching bag in the gym. That was the first time I ever experienced physical abuse from a man. After that, I quickly gathered my belongings and flew one-way back to Chicago from Las Vegas, forgetting that I ever knew this man. Now turning eighteen at the time, transitioning into womanhood, I lacked understanding, guidance, direction and still love.

Something about this love thing, I did not understand. It conflicted with my overall intelligence, focus and common sense. Ever since I can remember, I had a strong desire to love and be loved by a man. Some believe that my struggles in this area exist because I did not know my father for the first thirteen years of my life. Then there are those that say I am just a loving person who is cursed with loving too hard. Every person has a lesson to be learned. I learned numerous lessons yet still found myself making the same mistakes in my relationships.

One of my downfalls is that I subconsciously compromised my self-worth by trying too hard to make a wrong relationship work. I found myself doing things I thought a woman should do in a relationship. Aside from the fact that I was entirely too young to engage in such relationships, the problem with what I was doing was that I catered to men who did not deserve my love and commitment. I was simply allowing myself to be taken advantage of. I was doing too much and constantly changing to adapt to each relationship. I say all this to say that some of us are so quick to make changes for a man or woman but we are hesitant, reluctant and downright resistant to change for God.

Change is not always easy. There is a stripping away of the familiar and a need to embrace the unfamiliar. Many of us have defined ourselves according to our place in the natural world. We measure our worth by what our friends, family and significant others think of us. We measure our success by how much money we have, where we live or what we drive. Then God enters the picture and asks seemingly strange things of us. He changes our purpose from selfish to selfless. Now we have to start living for Him and doing things for the benefit of others. We start out our Christian walk excited and thinking we are ready for transformation, but when it comes, it brings uneasiness and is at times difficult to accept. Change does that.

In my search for love, I felt as if there was a stripping away of my identity that caused me to feel lost. I did not know who I was or whose I was. It never dawned on me that I had made my entire life about chasing after love. A void that I would later learn that only Jesus could fill.

John 15:9-17 (ESV)

As the Father has loved me, so have I loved you. Abide in my love. If you keep my commandments, you will abide in my love, just as I have kept my Father's commandments and abide in his love.

These things I have spoken to you, that my joy may be in you, and that your joy may be full. "This is my commandment, that you love one another as I have loved you.

Greater love has no one than this, that someone lay down his life for his friends. You are my friends if you do what I command you. No longer do I call you servants, for the servant does not know what his master is doing; but I have called

Cynthia Evans

*you friends, for all that I have heard from
my Father I have made known to you.
You did not choose me, but I chose you and
appointed you that you should go and bear
fruit and that your fruit should abide, so
that whatever you ask the Father in my
name, he may give it to you. These things I
command you, so that you will love one
another.*

Matthew 6:24

No man can serve two masters: for either he will hate the one, and love the other; or else he would hold to the one, and despise the other. Ye cannot serve God and mammon.

The Power of Fear

My search for love had me believing that I was not afraid of anything. I dove into relationships heart first. I trusted and believed in any and every one I was involved with until they would give me a reason not to anymore. Even when they proved themselves untrustworthy, I remained at their side for as long as they would have me. Truth be told I hung around even when they did not want me anymore. I realize now that I was afraid of rejection. It has been hard to accept not being wanted or needed. Fear of rejection also caused me to lose myself. I had trouble being and staying who God called me to be because I was too busy trying to be what I believed each man wanted me to be. It eventually became obvious to me that not having my father in my life affected my relationships. This part of my life I cannot retrieve, so I have had to deal with the reality that my dad was not there and realize that it was part of God's plan and was for a good reason.

Yet the fear of rejection caused a great deal of disturbances in my life. At some point, I felt pulled to talk to my dad about his absence, which was odd because up until then neither of us had ever mentioned it to one another. I did not understand that I needed to address this issue with him in order to help me make healthier decisions in my future relationships with other men. When I was finally drawn to do so, I did just that.

After accepting my father in my life for so many years without having *the talk*, I finally found the nerve to confront him. I started by first coming to grips with how I felt about not having my father around. Honestly, I did not know where to begin. I have loved my father ever since I could remember, even though I did not know who he was because he left me from my birth. Still I loved my daddy or at least the idea of daddy. I longed for the day that he would accept me into his life. I never hated him for neglecting me and I never really threw it in his face until about two or three years after I met him. I do not regret accepting my dad the way that I did, but I do regret allowing men into my life that same way. Regardless of what men from past relationships did to me, I forgave them and accepted them right back into my life when I should have just forgiven them and let them go. Looking back I guess I can say that maybe I did not despise daddy back then because I had not lived my life long enough to realize the difference he could have made. So, let me say this now:

"Daddy, I hate that you have cursed me to desire a man that wants nothing to do with me. I am repulsed that you were able to go on with your life for so long without me in it. I despise the feeling of being rejected by men that I have loved even though they did me wrong. I hate that I had to come looking for you before you came to look for me. I am disgusted that I have been so forgiving of a man just because I did not want him to leave me. I hate that a man could just sit up in my face

and tell me that he loves me when his actions have shown differently.

I hate that I sat around time after time and waited for a man to love me the way I loved him. I hate that I missed having a dominant, caring, loving and supportive male role model in my life. I hate that I could not control the way that I loved because all my life, all I ever wanted was to be accepted and loved by you.

You were supposed to be there to tell me to stay away from those knuckleheaded boys. You should have been there to tell me that I was beautiful, intelligent and any man would be a fool to pass me up. You should have been there to help me keep focused, set goals; teach me morals, values and self-respect.

Why were you not there?

I never told my dad those things until a few years ago because I was afraid that he would just lie to me like most men have, or that he would reject me once again. Fear of rejection will have us doing things that we should not or have us not doing what we should.

After a few more years of bumping my head, I began to learn my value and worth, got serious about my walk with the Lord and I married the man of my dreams. However, my love life before him was rocky to say the least.

I sometimes fear failure too. I failed to abstain from sex at an early age. I thought that in order to receive love I had to make love. When I lost my virginity at thirteen my understanding of love was that, you displayed it through sexual encounters. I did not understand the difference between love and lust. I did not think a man could love me without me having sex with him first. I failed at not having a baby before marriage. Back then, my thought process was that having the baby first would provide my man the incentive to get married. I failed in marriage with my first husband. I failed to realize and understand the dysfunction in my thinking and behavior. Even though I understood that the attitudes and behaviors I held were unhealthy and repeatedly took me out of God's will, I still failed to change them. I failed to finish many of the things that I have started. But most importantly, I failed at being a faithful servant to God. However, the one thing I love about the term *failed* is that it is in the past tense.

What was done in the past has been done and there is no need to indulge in self-pity, guilt and shame. Those are emotions designed by the enemy to keep us living in the past instead of living in the now and in faith for the future. The only thing the past proves is that it happened. It shows us what did not work and what we should not do again if we do not want the same results. However, once we have repented and asked God to forgive us for our wrong choices, bad decisions and behaviors, we turn from those things that are no more. *Micah 7:19* says, *He will turn again, he will have compassion upon us; he will subdue our iniquities; and thou wilt cast all their sins into the depths of the sea.*

Fear is crippling. Fear is debilitating. Fear keeps us from moving forward. It stunts our growth and then we wonder why we are always in the same place in our spiritual walk, or even worse, we are on a downward slope. We have to stop letting our emotions get the best of us. Since the enemy knows that I am a thinker and it is difficult for me to shut down my thoughts, he attacks me in my mind. He could bring up something that occurred ten years ago and I would respond as if it was happening right now, the same way that I negatively responded during that time. For so long I have fallen into this trap. As soon as the enemy begins to speak lies to you, talk right back to him. We have to silence the voice of the accuser, which is satan himself. *John 8:44 says, When he speaketh a lie, he speaketh of his own; for he is a liar, and the father of it.* Even when the enemy brings up the truth about what you have done, speak back to that too. Know that when you repent you are forgiven; believe that you are forgiven, turn from your wicked ways and walk in peace. Praise God for opportunities to grow and be successful! So what if we have not always done things the way they should have been done. As long as there is breath in our body and God is still on the throne, we still have a chance to get this thing going in the right direction.

We cannot continue to operate in the spirit of fear, the spirit of selfishness or defeat. Yes, we will make mistakes but who does not make mistakes? Yes, our feet may slip, we may stumble and fall, but who has not done that, too? Surely, we are not the first to be conflicted in our walk and we will not be the last, but we will continue to get up and walk. The Lord said that He would never leave us nor forsake us. We can take the scenic route, see the world and hope that we get to our destination of purpose before we leave this life and meet our judgment. Keep in mind that the judgment is real. On the other hand, we can go the *Jesus route*, endure the process and reap the harvest. I want double for my trouble.

Fear of rejection can be just as crippling. But in Christ what are we afraid of? Some of us were *'bout it, 'bout it* in the world? We were bold, confident, authoritative and then some. It was nothing for us to stand up for what we believed in and dared anybody to challenge us and tell us differently. Yet, we come into the house of God and we hide behind shyness and claim that we are being humble and meek. We try to avoid being noticed and we are definitely not trying to be heard. We are in and out, up and down, neglecting the fact that someone needs us to stand up and be consistent in Christ. Someone needs us to walk and speak boldly on Christ's behalf. People need to know that despite the strongholds and challenges of life that we all possess, God's grace allows us to still operate in His Kingdom.

People are crying out in need of a sign from God. They are praying for someone to tell them that they have not been forgotten; that He cares. They are hoping that someone will discern that they are hurting, afraid, confused and feel alone. Yet in our desire to fly under the radar, we neglect to see them. Then even if we do notice them and feel God's call to minister to them, we act as if we are afraid to speak into their life or we are too busy, but we welcome others to speak a word into our lives. We seek someone to tell us what God said about us so we can move. Not only do we not want to be accountable for ourselves, but also we do not want to be accountable for anyone else. Accountability is not our adversary. Being accountable for our actions helps us to operate decently and in order. Whether we choose to believe it or not we are held accountable when we do the right thing and we do not.

Romans 8:15

For ye have not received the spirit of bondage again to fear; but ye have received the Spirit of adoption, whereby we cry, Abba, Father.

1 Corinthians 6:9-12

Know ye not that the unrighteous shall not inherit the kingdom of God? Be not deceived: neither fornicators, nor idolaters, nor adulterers, nor effeminate, nor abusers of themselves with mankind, Nor thieves, nor covetous, nor drunkards, nor revilers, nor extortioners, shall inherit the kingdom of God.

And such were some of you: but ye are washed, but ye are sanctified, but ye are justified in the name of the Lord Jesus, and by the Spirit of our God.

All things are lawful unto me, but all things are not expedient: all things are lawful for me, I will not be brought under the power of any.

Worldly Pleasures

The Word of God says that *we are in the world but we are not of the world.* After I was saved, I did not get that memo. I did not just crave worldly relationships and recreational sex; I also enjoyed drinking. I would say *It is hard to stay saved because I like to party and the only people having fun are the ones in the secular clubs.* I can confess to having attended a whole lot of gatherings where you had better believe no one was thinking about Jesus. In fact, the only time some of us would reverence the Lord is the, *Oh, God!* we exclaimed during sex. Or, when we prayed to make it home safely after a night that left us in a drunken stupor. You know the prayer that went, *Lord, if you get me home safe this time, I promise the next time I will drink in moderation.* I kept my word too; I drank until I was moderately drunk again. Thank God for His grace because many of us should be dead. I know the Lord kept me.

I thank God that I can testify today of how He covered me through every red light that I ran; every white line that I swerved back and forth across while driving; every black out; and the car crash that could have taken my life and every person in the other vehicle. He was there covering me every time I had unprotected sex and when I almost got married to someone that alcohol had me convinced that I could spend the rest of my life with.

I do not know where I would be without the Lord who was on my side.

I am learning that just because we are Christians does not mean that we cannot have a good time, but there are boundaries. Boundaries that God placed in our spirit to protect us from hurt, harm and danger. I still trip out when I am with other Christians hanging out until the wee hours of the night. *Who does that other than heathens?* I would often say. My flesh was accustomed to binge drinking, strip pole dancing or having wild sex with the *flavor of the month* between the hours of eleven o'clock at night and six o'clock in the morning. If it were a good night, I would find another club, lounge, or even a strip club to continue feeding my flesh. Not much was off limits. As I am beginning to spend more time fellowshipping with my fellow sisters and brothers in Christ, I am adjusting a little better to the *saved* life. In other words, it does not seem so weird and boring anymore. Although very different from what I had become used to, I thank God that I can make the switch.

It is clear that for those who need to escape from the influences of the world, a change of environment and scenery may be necessary, but it does not have to become boring. I have shared some of the best times in my walk with those of like faith. No one needed a designated driver. No one passed out from drinking or drugging all night. No fights broke out, just a little *heated fellowship* when it came to the competition of the games we played. Now this was a prime example of *unworldly* fun. It may take some time though for the real hard partiers like me to adjust to new concepts of fun and excitement. Some of us have believed for a long time that fun, more than less, equates to sex, drugs and rock and roll. The Bible says in *2 Corinthians 5:17, Therefore if any man be in Christ, he is a new creature: old things are passed away; behold, all things are become new.*

Ain't No Party like a Holy Ghost party. Praise and worship draws God nearer. He dwells in the midst of our praise. There is no need to act as if you are someone that you are not. You do not have to front as if you are living large and in charge when most of the time you do not even know where your next dollar is going to come from. We can be completely naked before God. We can tap so far in to His presence that He takes us beyond the veil.

Is partying in secular settings a sin? Well, not necessarily, but oftentimes it is the guilty pleasures we engage in that come along with the partying that brings about the sin. For instance, flirting and acting as if you are single when you are married; or bumping and grinding on someone when you know that behavior is feeding your lust. How about drinking and getting drunk, even though that may not be your intention? Whatever crack we give the enemy to come in through, he is going to bust it wide open. Before you know it, we need to repent yet again. It is time out for repenting over the same things.

Many of us are not baby saints anymore. We cannot keep sipping on Similac when God wants to give us meat. If you, like me, love a good party, then we have to find ways to enjoy ourselves without falling into a trap. Granted there have been times when I have gone out clubbing and did not have even one drink.

Nevertheless, most of the time when I went out I did end up drinking an alcoholic beverage or beverages. I set myself up to fail and that was not to the devil's credit; it was my own fault. I made the conscious decision to drink alcohol and tamper with the ideas of my lustful fantasies. Yes, alcohol can do that. It can have you thinking that it is ok to do things that later on you will regret. I believe that people have an innate tendency to do what they think makes them feel good, and for me, it was drinking and clubbing. I love to dance and I *loved* to drink.

I drank for a number of reasons. During many of my adult years, alcohol had been the way I obtained my self-satisfaction. I drank alcohol in an attempt to escape reality and although alcohol was not able to remove the reality I wanted to escape, it made me feel good in spite of it for at least the moment. It seemed to me that alcohol temporarily repressed or dulled my emotions. For instance, when I needed to rid myself from the boredom of day-to-day living, minimize pain caused by a physical condition or relationship situation, deal with anxiety over the unknown, get relief from the stress of finances, or to overcome confusion, rejection, and denial of a hurtful reality; I would drink. In either case, alcohol provided me a more pleasant *feeling.*

In my religious response, I can easily say that I have chosen to give up alcohol because *my body is the temple of the Most High God* and I have a mandate to handle my temple with care. Yet if I could be transparent with you as I have tried to maintain throughout this text, I would say that I really chose to give up alcohol this last time because I felt the need to examine my triggers and to be obedient to the conviction in my own spirit. I chose to give up alcohol in an attempt to adopt alternatives that will help me deal with my emotions and reality in a healthier manner than I have in the past. My intention has been to learn better ways of coping with issues.

I had to make changes because of the responsibilities I carry and the character I hope to build for myself. It has become important for me not to in any case rely on alcohol. I want to live a life in which alcohol does not dictate the way I deal with the issues of life, or affect my behavior and how I treat those around me. I want to be able to sit before those struggling with alcoholism as an example that alcohol does not have to control their lives and that God will help them to stay clean and sober if that is their desire.

Because of refraining from alcohol, I realized the power of choice. It felt good to make what for me was the right decision not to drink. Every day I have to make a conscious decision to *just say no*. I have to believe, truly believe, that all things present in my life are working together for my benefit. Sometimes we have to endure things that are uncomfortable in order to grow, to learn and to mature in Christ.

I like to think I am genuinely real. In other words, what you see is what you get. I can appreciate when a person is honest about where they are in their walk with God. I recall watching a reality TV show of a known actor. *Yes, I sometimes*

> **Ephesians 5:18**
> *And be not drunk with wine, wherein is excess; but be filled with the Spirit;*

watch reality television. During this particular episode, the actor had the opportunity to speak with a First Lady of a mega church. The actor told First Lady straight up that she likes to have a drink, drop it like it's hot and have sex (by the way, she, the actor, was single at the time). She wanted to know specifically what she could and could not do according to the Word of God. I was glued to the television just waiting to hear the First Lady's response. I loved the authenticity of the actor's question and even more, I loved the response that she was given. In regards to the question asked about drinking, First Lady's response was quite simple. *You are a grown woman; you do what you want to do.* I thought *she is right.* We are always waiting for somebody we respect to tell us what we can or cannot do according to the Word of God instead of taking up our issue with God ourselves or accepting the scriptures at face value. I constantly struggled with the same question about drinking, often wondering, *Well can I drink or not?*

The Bible says that all things are lawful, but it also says to be sober. The dictionary defines sober as *not be drunk, to be serious and to be restrained.* Being sober allows us to be clearheaded, to use better judgment and to have a reasonable amount of self-control. A number of drugs can influence our behavior. Regardless, it is good for us to be sober, free from whatever one's drug of choice is.

I feel convicted if I consume alcohol no matter the amount. Since I have a relationship with God, I have to trust that it is the Holy Spirit causing the disturbance in my spirit if I drink and for *my* own good. You are probably thinking that I still did not answer the question of whether it is right to drink or not and you are right. Personally, when the Bible says to do *all* things in moderation I do not take that to mean consume alcohol or other drugs in moderation. I stand to be corrected, but I believe there is only one scripture in the Bible that talks about moderation. *Philippians 4:5 says, Let your moderation be known unto all men. The Lord is at hand.* Now how could I infer that we can drink in moderation from this scripture? In keeping the covenant; *Deuteronomy 29:6 says, Ye have not eaten bread, neither have ye drunk wine or strong drink: that ye might know that I am the Lord your God.*

Isaiah 28:7 speaks of the leaders,

...they are out of the way through strong drink; they err in vision; they stumble in judgment.

You may also be saying, *Well they drank wine in the days of old.* OK, well let us examine how that worked out for some of them.

1Kings 16:9-10;

And his servant Zimri, captain of half his chariots, conspired against him, as he was in Tirzah drinking himself drunk in the house of Tirzah. And Zimri went in and smote him, and killed him, in the twenty and seventh year of Asa king of Judah, and reigned in his stead.

Recall *Genesis the 19th chapter* when Lot's daughters conspired to get pregnant by their father in an attempt to preserve their bloodline since they no longer had husbands of their own. In verse 32, they said:

Come, let us make our father drink wine, and we will lie with him, that we may preserve seed of our father.

Regardless of how some of us twist or manipulate the scripture to justify our actions, we have to remember that as men and women of God we have a charge. According to *Titus 2:1-8*, it is our Christian duty to:

Speak thou the things, which become sound doctrine:

That the aged men be sober, grave, temperate, and sound in faith, in charity, in patience.

Aged women likewise, that they be in behaviour as becometh holiness, not false accusers, not given to much wine, teachers of good things;

That they may teach the young women to be sober, to love their husbands, to love their children, To be discreet, chaste, keepers at home, good, obedient to their own husbands, that the word of God be not blasphemed.

Young men likewise exhort to be sober minded. In all things shewing thyself a pattern of good works: in doctrine shewing uncorruptness, gravity, sincerity,

Sound speech that cannot be condemned; that he that is of the contrary part may be ashamed, having no evil thing to say of you.

Other than what the Bible speaks specifically of by scripture, I think it is difficult for any one person or group of people to tell anyone else *all* behaviors that are right or wrong. Each person has to assess their own actions and the consequences thereof to them and to others and consider how their relationship with God is affected. Ask yourself, *What has power over me?* Anything that has power over you rather than you having the power to *take it or leave it* needs to be re-evaluated.

Titus 2:11-13

*For the grace of God that
bringeth salvation hath
appeared to all men,
Teaching us that, denying
ungodliness and worldly lusts,
we should live soberly,
righteously, and godly, in this
present world;
Looking for that blessed hope,
and the glorious appearing of
the great God and our Saviour
Jesus Christ;*

The Cost of Disobedience

The second chapter of Judges talks about how even though the Lord had performed numerous signs and wonders and kept Israel from the hands of their enemies, Israel still did evil in the sight of the Lord. The Lord rose up Judges to deliver them out of the hands of those that spoiled them yet Israel continued to disobey the Lord's commandments.

Many of us make it appear so difficult to live for Christ, to live a holy life and to be righteous. Because sin was inherited from the infamous Adam and Eve we do have a sinful nature, and let us face it, it sometimes feels good to give in to certain urges. Yet the Holy Spirit gives us power over our flesh and the attacks of the enemy. In *Luke 10:19*, it says, *Behold, I have given unto you power to tread on serpents and scorpions and over **all** the power of the enemy, and nothing by any means shall hurt you.* The power of which the Lord speaks is an all-inclusive power. That means everything necessary for us to win in the battles of life lies within us through the power of the Holy Spirit.

Knowing this, why do many of us walk around accepting defeat in so many areas? At some point as we were sizing up our situation, the voice of deception came in and whispered a suggestion that the challenge we are facing is greater than what we are working with. Imagine that the serpent or scorpion is the lover who broke your heart into a million pieces or the financial debt that has risen above your ability to carry it. Imagine the serpent or scorpion lies between you and a college degree or a promotion at work or is in the way of your complete deliverance from whatever is oppressing you. According to the Word of God, your victory is attainable. Am I saying that satan has no power? No. Satan is powerful, he is diligent and he is persistent. God is fully aware of satan's tactics and his strong will. How do I know? Because realizing we could not fight life's battles on our own, He sent us His Holy Spirit that gives us power to overcome this enemy so we can live victoriously in spite of the fact that satan comes to *kill, steal, and destroy.* However, *Christ came that we might have life and have it more abundantly as expressed in John 10:10.*

A common tactic of the enemy is to make us forget what we have in Christ. Many of us repeatedly fall for this trick. I know there are times when the circumstances I face seem so difficult that I behave as though I do not even know God or as if His power has limits. Worry, doubt, impatience and fear take over my emotions and I begin to do the wrong things in an effort to bring about the right result. I find myself saying, *Oh, God is able. Yes. He can save, keep and deliver. He can create the world in seven days all by Himself but for this one, I am sure He could probably use my help.* I convince myself that in all of God's eternal existence He has never had to handle a situation like mine before. However, He has and He can.

Some of us who fall into this line of thinking believe that because we repeatedly fall short in our attempts to live righteously, our salvation is lost and God does not *want* to help us. Therefore, subconsciously, we would rather *not* believe that God can or will help in a given situation than to count on Him. We suffer from our own assessment that we are not worthy of God's time or effort. We accept defeat as well deserved or we take it upon ourselves to find our own way out – without *bothering* God. I think it is critical for me to explain that God does not play the kinds of games that we would play.

According to the Word of God when you complete the process of salvation, you repent and are baptized, filled with the power of the Holy Spirit, are sanctified and justified; there is no need to worry or wonder anymore about whose you are.

You belong to God and God has promised to never leave you nor forsake you. We are saved by the grace of God through our faith in Him. We have free and open access to God's throne of grace to obtain forgiveness. The enemy tries to get us to lose faith in God's desire or ability to come through for us just because we have miss-stepped or even fallen. God will not leave us but we can turn away from His open hands – and often do. However, to maintain coverage under the umbrella of that salvation we have to keep believing in Him.

Mark 16:16 says, *He that believeth and is baptized shall be saved; but he that believeth not shall be damned.* When we stop believing, we stop listening. When we stop listening, we stop obeying His commands. When we stop obeying His commandments, we slide back into our old sinful ways. When backsliding occurs, we walk away from the benefits of His care. Consider the child that has become *too grown* to live under daddy's roof. He no longer values daddy's advice, does not respect his rules, feels like he is big and bad enough to handle his business his way and decides that he can make it on his own. He still *loves* daddy and all, but daddy *just does not understand* that he has to be free to be himself. After going his way for a while, he realizes that daddy was actually trying to protect him from the cold cruel world out there and that it was good at home even <u>with</u> all the rules and responsibilities. You may turn away from God but home is always there for you. However, the rules remain in force. There is a charge to not only repent and receive forgiveness but to walk away from *practicing* sin.

In knowing the risks involved when God's grace is abused, why not just stop fighting against His will? There were times when I had been like the Israelites that repeatedly abused God's grace and mercy. In those times, God protected me from hurt, harm, and dangers that could have taken my life. For a while, I was grateful and showed my gratitude by staying away from those things that put me in jeopardy. Yet after a while, I found myself getting involved in those disastrous and dysfunctional behaviors all over again.

We lose so much ground when we are disobedient. The voices of *would have, could have, and should have* step in and leave us feeling bound when God declares that we are free. Ultimately, He has the upper hand anyway. An author once wrote *your arms are too short to box with God.* There have been times when I have fought against God's will and it only brought about more sorrow and weariness in my life. For instance, although my son is a blessing to me, having him out of wedlock has brought about a number of consequences.

His dad and I dated on and off during high school and I remember he was quite charming. I figured I would test the waters with him because we were around the same age and by this time it had become obvious to me that the older men I had been involved with were entirely too advanced for me. In dating older men, I found out quickly that I was not as mature for my age as I had thought I was because of what I had been told all my life, especially when it came to relationships. So I assumed that my son's dad would be more my speed. After having our child out of wedlock, I lived in fear that we would never get married. That fear caused me to behave in such a manner that I brought disgrace upon myself. I was so determined to share forever with him that I tolerated things I should not have.

I became obsessed with being able to say that we were still a couple and that our family unit was tight so much so that I would not admit the truth, which was that we did not belong together. The cost of my disobedience to the will of God just kept adding up all because I chose my will over the will of God. My son's father faced high costs too. He ended up with a psychotic *baby momma, ME.* He and I both put each other through drama; not only that, our son suffered too.

Oh yes, I will admit that I have some loose screws but thank God for His keeping power. This is not to say that all parents who have their children the *right way* and within God's structure for the family do not have their struggles. Not only did the relationship between my son's father and I not last after all, but now my son is forced to accept that he will never have both of his parents living under the same roof.

I was well aware of the fact that God's will was for a husband and a wife to create new life, not a boyfriend and a girlfriend. In spite of that knowledge, I chose to please man instead of pleasing God in an attempt to manipulate, control and try to save a relationship destined to fail because it was out of God's order in the first place. God's order gives us direction and purpose. When we fight against His order of things, we become hindered in our walk and that is what shacking up and playing house with my son's father and all of the other men in my past life has done, hindered me.

My hindrances have often come during my search for love. For instance, having sex out of wedlock was risky and sinful but I was not concerned about any of the dangers because it fed my irrational belief that giving up sex would ensure the man I loved would love me back. Your hindrance may not involve relationships. Some of you may be deterred in your walk with God in other ways.

Do You

Some people tend to get distracted and discouraged when looking at the progress of others in comparison to themselves. We can become discouraged if we start comparing our lives to what we see of the lives of fellow saints; those we *think* are so super holy and that they walk upright before the Lord at all times. When we consider our own inconsistencies and struggles, we conclude that we are not even worthy to be called righteous. What we see of them is that they are consistent, confident and unwavering in their faith and purpose. What we know of ourselves is that sometimes we do not come to church for weeks; we do not pray as we should; we do not read the Bible as we are supposed to; we don't know our purpose and we don't always *feel* saved. Either we are running to the Lord because the world ran us back into the church or we are running out of the church because it does not seem like we can live right. This comparison slows our progress because we tend to succumb to the thought that *if I cannot be perfect like they are I might as well not even try.*

In addition, as it relates to our progress, we must always keep a check on our motives. This walk is a walk of faith and trust in God and God alone. *Psalm 146:3* says, *Put not your trust in princes, nor in the son of man, in whom there is no help.* Certainly, we have to have confidence in our leadership but not so much so that they become the center of our motivation. If we do not build our relationship with God first, and put too much emphasis on pleasing leadership we may subconsciously make people in the position of power our gods. We must be careful not to give leadership a higher place of significance in our minds than they can live up to. Do not come to church and serve just because someone you respect in leadership suggested that you do so; do it because God called you to serve. Remember that our service is unto the Lord. Do not work diligently at a task to be liked or noticed, do it to the glory of God.

Not every ministry assignment offered to us is the assignment ordained for us. Prayerfully consider your commitment to any task or position. When we are serving in the wrong area, eventually we become frustrated, burned out and disillusioned with the position and with the leadership. My point is this; the enemy is always going to rear his ugly head when you are a child of God trying to do a work for God. As I am now finding my place in ministry and submitting myself to serve consistently, my goal is to please God because man is never *really* satisfied anyway. God is the one who qualifies us to perform an assignment. He is also the one who graces us to fulfill that assignment. Man may be the one who, at times, verbally appoints us, but God gives us the anointing.

Since the term anointing has been introduced, how often do we find ourselves saying things like, *Brother John or Sister Jane is so anointed. If I could just be like them, I would not keep backsliding.*

Please... God did not stop anointing and equipping people when He got to us. The same God that is blessing them wants to bless us too. What is also true, as quiet as it is kept, is that they have just as much of a struggle to keep themselves on track as we do. Paul even said in *1 Corinthians 9:27, But I keep under my body, and bring it into subjection: lest that by any means, when I have preached to others, I myself should be a castaway.* Sometimes they succeed and sometimes they fail, just as we do. God wants us to be who He designed us to be. This is why He made us *fearfully and wonderfully* then gave us His Holy Spirit. He does not want us to be copycats of His other creations. God knew exactly what he was doing when He created us. Although we are similar to other Christians in the sense that God made us all in His image and after His likeness, we are yet and still unique.

Walk in your originality by allowing God to continue to shape and mold you into the man or woman of God that He created you to be. You are God's original plan. Who is the one who will meet us on the Day of Judgment and make us give an account for our works on the earth? It is God not man. Does this mean that we have to become walking Bibles? No. Nevertheless, we should study the Word of God for ourselves since it is our guide, the blueprint for our Christian life and our daily bread. However, we do not need to be *so heavenly bound that we are no earthly good.* It is not that deep but it is that serious.

What is also serious and very real is our flesh. It is something that the Bible warns us that we must kill daily. In *Romans, Chapter 7:19,* Paul spoke, *For the good that I would I do not: but the evil which I would not, that I do.* No man is exempt from sin but ultimately, we still have a choice. We have to choose to die to self.

There is no need for me to tell you what the consequences of not dying to self are. We wonder why we are so caught up in our own mess. It is because we will not give ourselves away to God and allow Him to have His way. Allowing God to have His way is inviting Him into our life and our circumstances. The Bible says in Proverbs

James 4:7

Submit yourselves therefore to God. Resist the devil, and he will flee from you.

James 4:8

Draw nigh to God, and he will draw nigh to you. Cleanse your hands, ye sinners; and purify your hearts, ye double minded.

3:6, *In all thy ways acknowledge him, and he shall direct thy paths.* We have to seek God for direction instead of doing it our own way. In return, He gives us wisdom and understanding, two important concepts we need to have in this Christian walk. We fight, we kick and we wear ourselves out because there is no defeating God. He has all power in His hands. Why must we keep trying to run and hide? Do we really think that God does not see us or cannot find us? Whether we hide in alcohol, drugs, promiscuity, unbelief or whatever it may be, our whereabouts and our state of being is well known to God.

Did we learn anything from rebellious Jonah who had to spend three nights in the belly of the fish? *Come out Adam...show yourself Eve. Who told you that you were naked? Adam there is ground to be tilled. There is dominion to take.* The kingdom of God needs us working in the will of the Lord. Like the Virgin Mary who carried Jesus in her womb, there is purpose in our belly as well. The contractions seem unbearable. The labor pains seem never-ending but if we would just breathe and push through each pain, each disappointment, each failure, each shame, the guilt, the heartache and whatever else that may come during the process of the birth; we will bring forth fruit.

Psalm 55:22

Cast thy burden upon the LORD, and he shall sustain thee: he shall never suffer the righteous to be moved.

These are all the things that I have given unto the Lord: pain, disappointment, failures, shame, guilt and heartaches. I have cast these cares and burdens to Him; yet I am still reminded of them. Maybe these are just thorns designed to keep me humble and mindful of where the Lord has brought me from. I like to call them my contractions during the labor process. They are sometimes long and close together or short and far apart. No matter the course, they hurt. One thing about being pregnant is that not everyone will experience their pregnancy the same way but everyone has to push or be cut in order to bring forth the fruit.

Do you know what you are carrying in your belly? Many of us know what is inside of us. We know what God has spoken into our lives and that is why we run. We think the task is bigger than we are; and it is. I am a dreamer. I can remember vividly two dreams in particular that shook me to my bone. I believe they were revelatory dreams. One of the dreams revealed to some extent one of the ways the Lord intends to use me. In this particular dream, I was on a platform standing before a mass of people and speaking God's word. I am thinking, *really, Lord? You are 'sum thin' else. Why me? You know what I have done. You know what people would think of me. What can I say? How will I defend myself from the attacks, because surely people are going to judge me? People that I have partied with, smoked with, drank with, slept with and done ill with. Look at how many of our leaders have fallen in the public eye. Who would want to come under that kind of scrutiny?* Then I am reminded of *Jeremiah 1:5-8* where it says,

> *Before I formed thee in the belly I knew thee; and before thou camest forth out of the womb I sanctified thee, and I*

ordained thee a prophet unto the nations.
Be not afraid of their faces: for I am with
thee to deliver thee, saith the LORD.

At some point, we have to stop allowing our past to dictate our future. We even have to stop allowing our present to dictate our future as well. You might believe our past disqualifies us, but I believe God is saying our past *pre-qualifies* us. Who better to speak to those who are going through the very things that God has brought us out of? If you witness another person stick a fork into an electrical socket and are electrocuted, do you also need to go stick a fork into a socket to know what the experience feels like? I appreciate the opportunity to learn from the mistakes of others instead of having to experience the pain first hand. Likewise, when someone is broke and down and out the last person they probably would want to hear from is someone who has been fed with a silver spoon all of their life. What would that individual know about being broke, busted and disgusted? What would they know about sleeping in cars or under bridges in the heat of the summer or the cold of the winter with no place to go or having no one to turn to? What would that person know about not having any money to feed his or her family or pay the bills? The one who has been through what I am going through and has come out on top is whom I need to hear a word of encouragement from. Their testimony alone may be the difference between me wanting to seek the Lord for my help and me walking away with no hope.

In a separate dream, God sent a well-known man of God to inform me that I was still pregnant with purpose and that

I had not aborted my gift. It came during a familiar season, the one in which I often think that God has given up on me and has taken back that gift He placed in my belly. I had given up. I had lost hope. I figured it was pointless to keep thinking that God would use me in any way to make a difference in anyone else's life. Most of the time I could not even keep myself on the right track.

Apparently, God can trust us with our gifts even when we do not trust ourselves with them. *His ways are not our ways, and His thoughts are not our thoughts. Jeremiah 29:11* says, *For I know the thoughts that I think toward you, saith the LORD, thoughts of peace, and not of evil, to give you an expected end.* We have to stop trying to figure out what God is doing, run back into his arms and trust the process. Instead of doing just that our tendency is to come up with every excuse in the world.

Exodus 4:10

And Moses said unto the Lord, O my Lord, I am not eloquent, neither heretofore, nor since thou hast spoken unto thy servant: but I am slow of speech, and of a slow tongue.

Exodus 4:11

And the Lord said unto him, Who hath made man's mouth? Or who maketh the dumb, or deaf, or the seeing, or the blind? Have not I the Lord?

Exodus 4:12

Now therefore go, and I will be with thy mouth, and teach thee what thou shalt say.

Excuses, Excuses

We have more excuses than Moses had when God told him to lead the Israelites out of Egypt. Even after God commanded Moses to go and assured him that he would be with him, Moses pleaded for the Lord to send his brother Aaron instead. I have had a ton of excuses. Here are just a few that I have used along with my personal revelations or experiences. See if any of them sound familiar.

I was stripped of my childhood. At a very young age I could vividly remember my life fade from great to good, from good to not so bad, from not so bad to *Why am I still living?* Elder family members try to encourage me to think back to when my childhood was normal. The times when my mother was an awesome single parent; the times I enjoyed my youth and was excited to be a kid. I have wished that I could remember those times. I see them in photos and I hear about them in family tales but what remains with me more than anything is the downfall, the struggle, the cry for help and the need for love.

When my mother was introduced to crack cocaine, I was inducted into motherhood. I had to grow up fast to take up her slack. It seems I went from eight to eighteen years old overnight. Because of this, my great-grandmother nicknamed me Ma. Everyone thought the name was cute because it had come to fit me so well. Not once did anyone stop to ask me how being called Ma at eight years old made me feel. Frankly, I never liked the nickname. My uncle and cousins teased me constantly. The adults could not even see that what they thought was a blush was really the look of shame and embarrassment. I was no longer known by my birth name, I had become known as Ma.

From eight to ten years old I witnessed my family go from having everything we needed to have nothing at all. It had gotten so bad that my maternal grandmother, who at the time, lived in another state had to send for me and become my guardian. She was outraged at hearing that her frail, but strong; tired, yet hopeful granddaughter had been put in the position to take on the responsibilities of parenting children, three to be exact. That is when I first developed the habit of removing myself from the difficult situations and moving on as if they never existed.

I did not understand it was a temporary solution. That misunderstood philosophy had become my way of living; running from my problems instead of facing them. Christ wants us to mature in Him. What we think are our obstacles, God sees them as opportunities and strengths. Because I grew up fast, I learned responsibility and accountability to family early. I learned how to parent children before having my own child. Therefore, when my son was born, at least I was ready and able to properly care for him.

I was not raised in the church. God used many people who were not raised in the church. It takes some people a lifetime of study and fellowship to develop a sense of God, His word and their purpose. However, this does not mean that God cannot work His plan in us and through us in a short period. Maybe it is good that we were not raised in church, because of our personal experiences and point of view, we can offer a different perspective. We may be able to reach those who need saving and who need to hear from someone who has been where they are. The message may need to come from someone who does not know the *traditional* things to say, but will say only what God has given them to say. Besides, sometimes *church folk* sugarcoat everything or act like their flesh has never given them any problem.

I do not know enough scriptures.
Well, I have a Bible. If you do, then

reading it is a good place to start. God has not required us to memorize every scripture in His word but grab hold to a few scriptures that have made a great impact on you, scriptures that you can recite, especially when the enemy is busy.

My character is flawed. Work on fixing it. We were designed to be shaped and molded. The clay is not dry yet. Locate the problem areas in your character, or lack thereof and improve them. God is not going to do it all for us but He will see us through. As stated in one of my favorite gospel songs by Leon Timbo *You might not be perfect but you are forgiven.*

Here is my favorite one. **Since God created me, He could just make me over again, all at once.** We want God to do so much for us but He requires some things from us too. He gave us his Holy

Spirit, the power to become the Sons of God.

People will not receive me. Not everyone received Jesus either. Take up your cross and keep it moving. They can deny us; they can even delay us; but they cannot stop us.

My parents were not good parents. My mother would feel so bad about her drug abuse that she basically allowed me to do just about anything I wanted to make up for it. Of course, it was also to keep me out of her way so she could get high without being bothered by her conscience. Soon as I figured out how vulnerable she was in that condition, I began to use her weakness to my advantage. That meant that even as a pre-teen I would hang out all hours of the night with my friends. Their mothers were out doing the same as mine or worse, so none of us really had any responsible adults to answer to. I was fatherless, virtually motherless, developing into eye candy and free as a bird. My parents were not the best during my upbringing, but my Father in Heaven, God, has been the best thing that has ever happened to me.

Please note that God does not want our excuses. He wants a willing vessel and a faithful servant. He wants us to *decrease so that He can increase.* He could have used anyone that He wanted but He chose you. We really need to get over ourselves. We have to stop thinking that God must have made a mistake when He called us to do a good work for Him. If we continue to wait until we have it all together then we will never be available to do the will of God. He wants to use every single one of us. God designed us with purpose in mind. *Philippians 1:6* says, *Being confident of this very thing, that he which hath begun a good work in you will perform it until the day of Jesus Christ.* He thinks more of us than we do of ourselves. God wants more from us because He knows what He has put into us. No more playing our victim card, it gets old after a while. People start to know your hand before you even play it and hate to see you coming.

I imagine the Lord must have gotten pretty sick of me using my *not having known my dad excuse* because after a while He dropped in my spirit the understanding that I was better off not knowing him during that time. I later wrote a short story entitled *Fatherless* that I would like to share with you. Many of us have grown up without a dad or father figure in our lives. For a short amount of time, I was blessed to have a man take on the role of a father to me. He and his family embraced me as if I were their own. Yet, I always knew that he was not my biological father. I yearned to meet the man with whom I shared the same blood. My father has never been emotionally or physically available and I noticed that the type of men that I would date were also emotionally and/or physically unavailable. Even after finally meeting my biological dad, I was still... fatherless.

Fatherless

In the Beginning

Imagine a little girl looking for her father. A man she never knew but was convinced that he had everything she needed. She searches the phone book for his name, dials every number and asks, *Is my daddy there?*

No one ever gives her the answer she seeks. Yet, she does not give up her search. She knows that he is out there because he created her. Her need to find him far exceeds the ridicule from family and friends who said that she is wasting her time and searching for someone who is nonexistent. She keeps looking for him so that he can at least tell her *I love you, I miss you, I want you* and *I need you.*

This little girl did all she knew to do and still could not find her father. One day the little girl finally gave up or so she thought, not knowing that subconsciously she looked for him in every male relationship she ever experienced. *Are you the one? You create things just as my daddy and you say you love me.* His actions form the clear reply *I am not the one.* Rejected but still hopeful, she continues her subconscious search. *Are you the one, because you are tall and slim, just like my daddy and you said that you missed me when I was away?* His deeds respond, *No, I am not the one.*

At some point in her life, she had heard someone say that she should never give up on her dreams. With that in mind, she continued seeking and pursuing for at least the one who said, *I want you, and I need you.* Moreover, she found him...,

"him" became them...and "them" became too many to count. She gave everything she had. She did everything she knew to do. Yet and still she never found the father she sought.

The emptiness became toxic to her spirit. Over time, that empty hole in her soul overflowed with pain and sorrow, bitterness and resentment, disappointments and doubts. All she wanted was her father. Instead, she remained...

Cynthia Evans

*F*atherless

*A*bandoned

mis *T*reated

c*H*eated

unappr*E*ciated

fo*R*gotten

mishand*L*ed

n*E*glected

dete*S*ted

indi*S*tinct

But, Better is the Ending of a Thing, than the Beginning

The little girl wept. As a teen, she wept. As an adult, she wept. Then one day somebody told her about a man named Jesus - and she wept even more.

Now she wept because she realized that Jesus is the one she had been searching for all along. He told her *He loved her, He missed her, He wanted her* and *He needed her.*

He told her that she has never been fatherless because He created her before the foundation of the world and has never left her nor forsaken her. Yes she was abandoned by her biological father, cheated out of a father/daughter relationship, unappreciated for the love she had to give, mishandled by those father substitutes, neglected by those who were charged with her care, detested by those who didn't know her story and at times, indistinct. However, these were all stepping-stones along the journey that were designed to lead her to the Father.

I love You, Daddy!

Think About It:

Have you ever wanted someone in your life so bad that you gave everything you had in your search to find him or her or your hope to be with him or her? You lost your identity because your life became centered on someone or something that altered the course of your journey. No longer were you seeking to find out who you were or your purpose in life. You were committed to finding what you thought you were missing and no one could stop you.

With that same passion, we should seek the Lord. He should be the head of our life and the reason we live, for He is the one who gave us life. We honor Him by living according to His word. He loves us to seek Him and to desire Him. He wants to be a part of our lives. Without Him we are not living, just merely existing.

God calls us a peculiar people. We are not ordinary; we are special. We are His beloved. His Holy Spirit dwells in us. When we operate in the divine power and authority He has given to us, we become world changers. I have to tell you that even though God burst my *fatherless* bubble by making me see that He was my Father all along, I still found another excuse and another and so on, but excuses are just crutches.

They become tools that we use for manipulation to gain some sort of sympathy or to avoid fulfilling our purpose. I am tired of acting as if I am the weakest link when I have the DNA of Christ. There is nothing weak about God. He is our strong tower. Have you noticed the key person in each of these excuses? They are *I, My* and *Me.* We become so focused on ourselves that we miss what God is trying to do in and through us. We become selfish and self-centered and there is no room to serve God's people when we are consumed with ourselves. Give yourself away.

2 Corinthians 5:10

For we must all appear before the judgment seat of Christ; that every one may receive the things done in his body, according to that he hath done, whether it be good or bad.

Cynthia Evans

Epilogue

Looking Back

Luke 9:62

And Jesus said unto him, No man having put his hand to the plough, and looking back, is fit for the kingdom of God.

Many of us have the tendency of going *Back down memory lane* but sometimes reminiscing can be a trap if you have not addressed the issues and healed from the situation, or from who or what it is you are thinking about. We know that our words have power. *Death and life is in the power of the tongue... Proverbs 18:21.* However, our thoughts can be just as powerful. For instance, a single person who has struggled with not having sex out of wedlock begins to think about someone they had been sexually involved with and how pleasurable the experience was for them. Now the individual finds him or herself putting their thoughts into action. They have gone from thinking about having sex (planted seed in thoughts), to now making the phone call (watering the seed) and arranging to meet. Next thing you know, he or she is back at the altar repenting again over the same deed they have been at the altar repenting about before.

This is why when certain people, places and things pop back up, which if you are human they will; we have to stop looking back. We have to remember what our expected end is; and that is to be with the Lord in everlasting life. We have to remember why we walked away from our old ways in the first place. We were no longer content in our sins, realizing that we are better than what we displayed in our past life. We have grown up in Christ. We have self-esteem and confidence now and are no longer needy because our Father supplies all our need. We are no longer beggars for love and

> **Psalms 37:24**
>
> *Though he fall, he shall not be utterly cast down; for the Lord upholdeth him with his hand.*

acceptance. We no longer fear rejection because we know that we are accepted in Christ. We must hold on to on to these things. These are the things that we have to believe. Otherwise, our flesh wins and we end up on the same merry-go-round that already seems to have taken forever for some us to get off.

I do not know what your strongholds or your obstacles may be, but I do know that they are only footstools that can take you to a higher level in Christ. *What the enemy meant for evil God meant it for our good.* Footstools are the places where the enemy dwells and conspires against us. We have to know that footstools were designed for us to place our feet on top of them. Even though at times we may fall back a few steps when we lose our balance (backslide), we can still rise above what is intended to be beneath us.

Footstools have their benefits. They allow us to go a step farther, a step higher and they can give us balance. Instead of slumping down on our footstools and getting comfortable, we have to rise above them, step on top of them and move forth. The Word says *the steps of a good man are ordered by the Lord.* Satan's desire is for us to think that we have no power. He wants us to believe that because we have fallen back, made mistakes and bad choices repeatedly that God will never receive us again. He wants us to think that we can never go back home to God. But the devil is a liar. Thank God for His grace and mercy! No matter what anyone says, we cannot allow him or her to make us think or feel that God will not receive us again. Unlike many of our natural parents, God will not close the door on us. He will not kick us out and change the lock. We will always have the keys to tap in to His presence when we submit ourselves unto Him.

There will always be people who will never let us live down our past but just because they think we cannot change does not mean that we will not or have not changed. We have to come back home to our Father's house - the house of the Lord and the will of the Lord. We must remember what He says about us. He calls us the apple of His eye, His beloved. He has redeemed us and has forgiven us of ALL of our sins according to *Colossians 1:14*. The following was adapted from a bookmark from the Church at South Las Vegas titled *I AM*. Affirm these things within you continually.

I Am

I Am Significant...

I am the salt and the light of the earth.

I am a branch of the true vine,

a channel of His life.

I have been chosen and appointed to bear

fruit.

I Am Secure...

I am free from condemning charges against

me.

I cannot be separated from the love of God.

I have been established,

anointed and sealed by God.

I Am Accepted...

I am God's child.

I have been justified.

I have been bought with a price.

I belong to God.

We have already tasted and seen
that *the Lord is good and that his mercy
endureth forever.* We have been filled with
His Spirit. No one or no-thing has ever
made us *feel* like He has. He shows His
love daily. He feeds us daily. He forgives
us daily. New mercies we see daily. Who
else can show us this type of favor? No
one but the Lord. Remember when you
were first saved. You sought after Him like
no other. He wants us to reignite the fire
so we can go higher in Him. Simply put,
There is No Place like Home. I want to be
taken up in the clouds, crowned by my
heavenly Father and walk the streets
paved with gold.

Luke 15:22

But the father said to his servants, Bring forth the best robe, and put it on him; and put a ring on his hand, and shoes on his feet:

Luke 15:23

And bring hither the fatted calf, and kill it; and let us eat, and be merry:

Luke 15:24

For this my son was dead, and is alive again; he was lost, and is found. And they began to be merry.

About the Author

If there were only one word used to describe Cynthia Evans it would be resilient. Having endured varying degrees of storms and numerous seasons in her life thus far, she has been inspired to share her intriguing testimonies through literary expressions in hope that they will minister to and encourage the hearts of her readers. Her style varies from poetry, which is expressed in pieces such as *Chemistry* or *All in My Head*, to short stories such as *Fatherless*, all of which can be found within the chapters of this book *Voices of Cyn...Traces of a Backslider.* This compelling work speaks to those of us who struggle to make the right choices while navigating through the dysfunctions in our relationships and enduring the consequences of yesterday's bad decisions. The readers embark on a journey with Cynthia that carries them out onto the road to hell and back home again.

Cynthia was born in Chicago, Illinois and spent most of her life in between her hometown and Las Vegas, Nevada. A single mother at the age of twenty-one now in her third year of marriage, she persevered and achieved her Bachelor of Science degree in Human Services Counseling with a minor in Addictions Treatment and is currently working toward her Master's degree in Marriage and Family Therapy. She bears many titles: servant of God, wife, mother, grandmother, student and now author. Since the age of sixteen, when she initially found Christ and accepted Him into her life, Cynthia has struggled to find her own purpose and place in the Kingdom. Like many of her readers, she found herself vacillating in and out of the church for years as she yielded to the various tricks and temptations of the enemy. Nevertheless, she can now proudly proclaim that her purpose has been revealed and she is rooted and grounded in Christ and has submitted to the will of the Lord for her life.

Cynthia declares to the world that she is nothing more than a sinner saved by grace and gives all glory and honor to God Almighty for His mercy, grace and favor over her life. The fact that God endured all of her escapades and double-mindedness during her journey so far is a testimony of His faithfulness to complete the work He starts within each of us. Also knowing that the journey is by no means over and that there are tripping tendencies in her flesh from which she still must be freed, she is prepared to be further purged and used by God for His glory.

Jeremiah 3:12

Go and proclaim these words toward the north and say, Return thou backsliding Israel saith the LORD; and I will not cause mine anger to fall upon you: for I am merciful saith the LORD and I will not keep anger forever.

Let's Connect

www.VOICESOFCYN.com

Twitter.com/VOICESOFCYN

Facebook.com/VOICESOFCYN

Myspace.com/VOICESOFCYN

NCM PUBLISHING PRESENTS

NCM PUBLISHING PRESENTS

A GENERATION
of *Curses*

A NOVEL BY

Patricia A. Bridewell & Faatima Albasir-Johnson

CPSIA information can be obtained at www.ICGtesting.com
Printed in the USA
BVOW022118050212

282114BV00005B/3/P

9 780983 346142